## A Discovery Biography

# Frederick Douglass

— ◆ —

### *Freedom Fighter*

by Lillie Patterson
*illustrated by Gray Morrow, except pages 11 and 19 by
Daniel Mark Duffy*

**CHELSEA JUNIORS**
*A division of Chelsea House Publishers*
*New York ◆ Philadelphia*

This book is for Aunt Frances and Uncle Al

The Discovery Biographies have been prepared under the
educational supervision of Mary C. Austin, Ed.D,
Reading Specialist and Professor of Education, Case
Western Reserve University.

Cover illustration: Daniel Mark Duffy

First Chelsea House edition 1991

1  3  5  7  9  8  6  4  2

ISBN 0-7910-1410-X

# Contents

# Frederick Douglass: Freedom Fighter

# Chapter *1*

# Grandma Betsey's Fred

Fred woke suddenly from a sound sleep. Someone leaned over his pallet in the darkness.

"Sh!" the woman whispered softly. "It's your mamma."

Fred hugged her. "Can you stay with us this time, Mamma Harriet?"

"No, son. But I had to see you, if just for a little while." She smoothed Fred's curly black hair and kissed him.

Her cheeks were wet with tears. "Don't forget me, honey. And don't ever forget your name: Frederick Augustus Washington Bailey. It's a grand name. It was all I could give you."

Fred had seen his mother only a few times in his seven years. Harriet Bailey was a slave and worked on a plantation twelve miles away. To see Fred, she had to walk twelve miles after working in the fields all day. She had to walk the long way back to be in the fields by sunup.

Fred lived with his grandmother, Betsey Bailey. She did not work in the fields, but cared for the small children of slave mothers. Her cabin sat at the edge of a plantation on the Eastern Shore of Maryland.

The morning after his mother's visit, Fred helped Grandma Betsey in her vegetable garden.

"Grandma?"

"Yes, Fred."

"Why can't Mamma Harriet stay with us?"

"She has to do what Old Master tells her to do."

"Who is this Old Master you're always talking about?"

Grandma Betsey sighed. "I'll tell you about him one day."

"Tell me now, Grandma."

So Grandma Betsey sat under a tree and talked to Fred about slavery.

"The Old Master is Captain Aaron Anthony. He owns the mothers of the children here. He owns the children too."

Fred hugged his grandmother. "Well, he doesn't own me. I belong to you."

Grandma Betsey took Fred's face in her hands. "He owns me, you, this cabin, everything here. I hate to see you growing. Soon as you are able to work he'll take you away from me."

"No! No! Don't let him take me."

"Don't you worry, honey." Grandma Betsey looked into the bright spring sky. "Better days are coming for us."

That spring of 1824 passed into summer. Fred fished with Grandma Betsey as the two talked and sang together. He watched the boats with white sails and dreamed of sailing with them.

One morning Grandma Betsey took Fred's hand. "We're going for a walk."

They walked for miles. It was late afternoon when they came to a large plantation. They walked up a long drive, passed a big house and came to some small cabins. Children played about them.

"Go and play with the children," Grandma Betsey told Fred. Her face was sad. She hugged him hard and walked away without looking back.

Fred stayed with the children for a time. Then a little girl ran to him. "Grandma Betsey's gone. She left you."

"Grandma Betsey!" Fred screamed. He threw himself to the ground and sobbed. He knew now why he was here. His happy days with Grandma Betsey were over. It was time to go to work as a slave.

*Chapter* 2

# Great House Farm

Fred spent the next three weeks crying for Grandma Betsey and learning about the Lloyd plantation. Colonel Edward Lloyd was one of the richest men in Maryland. He owned over 1,000 slaves and many plantations. The Lloyd family lived in the big mansion on this farm. Slaves called it "Great House Farm."

The plantation was like a country village. Fred's owner, Captain Anthony, was manager of the Lloyd plantations. He, too, lived at Great House Farm.

Captain Anthony put Fred in one of the cabins under the care of an old cook. Fred swept the walks and yards. He chased chickens and ducks out of the gardens. He drove the cows from the pastures at sunset.

Great House Farm was beautiful. Fred loved its beauty, though he missed Grandma Betsey. But then something happened to make him hate the farm.

It was early morning. Fred awoke to the sound of screaming. He peeped through a big crack in the cabin. "It's the slave traders," someone cried. Fred crept outside to see better.

A mother hugged her little girl. "No!" she screamed. "You can't take her."

Then Captain Anthony pulled the child away.

The mother ran to the traders. "Oh, please! Buy me too. She's all I've got."

The buyers went on counting money. They paid several hundred dollars for each slave bought. Then they marched the slaves out of the yard.

"They're going to the deep South," the mother cried. "I'll never see my little girl again."

During the next months, Fred learned other horrors of slavery. He saw slaves whipped.

When Fred was eight, his mother died. No one told him she was sick. No one took him to see her.

"I hate slavery," Fred whispered every day.

He thought of the life in the Great House. The Lloyds ate the best foods. They dressed in silks and rode in fine carriages. They had dozens of servants.

Then he thought of life in the slave cabins. Slaves were packed together in these huts. They worked from sunup to sunset, in all kinds of weather. Their main food was cornmeal and fat meat or fish. The children all ate from a wooden tray, using oyster shells for spoons. Fred was always hungry.

Children under ten wore only a shirt that hung down to their knees. They never got shoes, stockings, pants, coats or blankets for cold weather. Fred had to sleep in a closet near the fireplace.

In winter he stuck his feet in the warm ashes to keep them from freezing.

*"Why am I a slave?"* Fred asked himself. *"Why are some people slaves and others masters?"*

One day Miss Lucretia came to visit her father, Captain Anthony. She was married, but everyone still called her Miss Lucretia.

She needed someone to run errands. Fred came. "What lively eyes you have!" she told him. "And such nice manners."

Fred helped her each day. Miss Lucretia liked to hear him sing. The two played a game. Whenever Fred was hungry, he stood under her window and sang. She would laugh and hand him bread and butter.

One day Miss Lucretia sent for Fred. "I have wonderful news," she said. "You're going to the city of Baltimore. My husband's brother needs someone to care for his little boy. Go and wash. I have a pair of pants for you."

"Oh, thank you!" Fred gave a whoop of joy and ran down to the river. He sang as he rubbed the dirt away. "I must be clean, must be clean for Baltimore."

Fred left that Saturday. As the boat sailed away, he looked back at Great House Farm. Then he turned his face toward Baltimore.

Great adventures lay ahead. Fred could feel it.

# Chapter *3*

# Baltimore and Books

Fred found Baltimore more exciting than he had dreamed. Fancy carriages rolled along the busy streets. Big ships came and left for places around the world. Tall red-brick buildings with white stone steps stood in rows.

His happy days with the Auld family began. He looked after young Tommy and ran errands. Mrs. Auld treated him almost as a member of the family.

One morning she said, "It's time to study your A B C's, Tommy. You may listen, Fred."

Each morning Fred listened and watched while Tommy learned. Soon he knew the A B C's as well as Tommy. Mrs. Auld began teaching them together. Soon they could put the letters together to spell words.

Mr. Auld came home one day during the lesson. "What is going on?" he asked angrily.

Mrs. Auld laughed. "I'm so proud of Freddy. He can read as well as Tommy."

"Stop this at once!" Mr. Auld shouted. "Never teach a slave to read. Once he can read he will want to be free."

Mrs. Auld stopped the teaching. But Fred did not stop learning. "I'll teach myself," he decided. He made friends with the white boys who lived nearby. He asked them questions about school. He found an old speller and studied in secret. The boys became Fred's teachers. The street became his schoolhouse.

By the time Fred was twelve, he could read very well. He watched for scraps of newspapers or magazines and hid them in his pocket.

Fred earned pennies helping friends shine shoes. When he had saved 50 cents he bought a book he had seen the others reading. *The Columbian Orator* was a book of speeches about liberty. Fred practiced the speeches aloud. He liked the grand thoughts about freedom.

Fred listened carefully when anyone talked about slavery. One day he heard Mr. Auld and friends talking angrily. "Those abolitionists are helping the slaves run away!"

Fred was excited. Who were the abolitionists? Did they really help slaves? He finally found his answer in an old newspaper. The abolitionists were people working to abolish, or end, slavery in the South. The northern states had already abolished slavery.

This news gave Fred hope. There were white men who hated slavery too. He kept on reading and writing in secret. And he began thinking about escaping to freedom.

# Chapter *4*

# "Let Me Be Free"

"Step lively, Fred! Work faster!"

Fred heard this from dawn to dusk. He was now sixteen and had a new owner. Captain Anthony was dead. So was Miss Lucretia. Fred belonged to Thomas Auld, Miss Lucretia's husband. He lived in St. Michaels, an oyster-fishing village down in Talbot County, Maryland.

Thomas Auld was mean to his slaves and never gave them enough to eat. He did not like Fred because Fred was not afraid to speak his mind.

"City life has spoiled you," Thomas Auld told Fred. "I'll have to send you to a slave-breaker."

Masters often sent troublesome slaves to slave-breakers. These men worked and whipped the slaves until they became easier to manage. So Fred went to the farm of Edward Covey.

Fred had never been a field slave. He did not know how to handle farm tools and animals. The first week Covey said, "Go get a load of wood. Take the cart and two oxen. Hurry!"

Fred finally got the load of wood. But the oxen ran away with the cart.

Fred did not know how to stop them. Crash! They ran into the gate, breaking cart and gate.

Covey dashed over to a tree and cut three long switches. "Take your clothes off," he ordered Fred.

Fred stood stubbornly, not moving.

Covey ripped Fred's clothes off. The switches made long red marks across Fred's skin. He clenched his teeth together and would not cry out or beg Covey to stop.

Over the next six months Covey whipped Fred at least once every week. Fred worked until he nearly dropped, in rain, snow, hail and heat. He grew silent. He never smiled.

Covey laughed. "At last I've broken him."

Early one morning Fred went to the barn to feed the horses. Covey sneaked up behind him with a long rope. Suddenly Freds' eyes flashed. Then he doubled his fist. He was seventeen now, tall and powerful.

"Are you going to resist me?" Covey asked.

"Yes, sir. I don't want to fight you, Mr. Covey. But I won't let you whip me this time."

Covey leaped at Fred like a tiger. But Fred was like a lion. He held Covey in his strong hands. The two began to give blow for blow. They rolled out of the barn door onto the ground. Covey finally gave up.

"I am a man," Fred told himself. "No master will ever whip me again."

Covey was ashamed to let people know that a young slave had beaten him. He did not report Fred to anyone. He was glad when Auld hired Fred out to another farmer.

On this farm Fred made close friends with other slaves. He taught them in secret to read. He talked to them about freedom.

Fred and five slaves decided to run away. "We'll borrow a canoe and paddle up Chesapeake Bay," Fred planned. "Then we'll go northward on foot. The night before Easter will be a good time."

"How will we know where we're going?" one slave asked.

"We'll follow the North Star. It will guide us to the free states."

On Saturday morning men with guns rode up to the farm. They had found out about the runaway plan. The slaves were put in jail.

"What will happen now?" Fred wondered.

The Aulds of Baltimore saved him. Hugh Auld begged his brother to send Fred back to him.

# Chapter *5*

# Escape

Fred went to work in a Baltimore shipyard. He learned quickly and soon became a skillful worker.

Every week Fred got paid. He could not spend the money, though. A slave's earnings belonged to his owner.

It was at the shipyard that Fred met Stanley, the sailor. Stanley was a free black. All blacks in the South were not slaves. Some were born free. Some were freed by kind masters. Some worked long years to buy their freedom.

"Every Sunday night the free blacks get together," Stanley told Fred. "We teach each other what we know. I'll take you to one of our meetings."

Fred went. Everyone liked him. He studied with the group each week. And he began walking home with one of the girls after the meetings. She was Anna Murray. Her calm face and long black hair made Fred think of an Indian princess.

One night Fred whispered, "I'll be free soon, Anna."

"How, Fred?"

"I have a plan. If you miss me, don't worry."

"Be careful, Fred. They'll kill you if you're caught."

Fred planned carefully, step by step.

First, he needed money. He got Auld to let him "hire out" his time. Owners sometimes let slaves pay them a sum each week, and keep for themselves any money left over. Fred worked early and late, Sundays and holidays.

One night Anna surprised him. She put some money in his hand. "Take it, Fred. I've been saving too. You find freedom. Then send for me."

Next, Fred needed "free papers." Free blacks had to carry papers to prove their freedom. Stanley had the answer. He offered Fred his "seaman's protection." "This paper protects black seamen anywhere," Stanley told Fred. "I'll lend you my sailor's suit and hat too. You can mail everything back to me later."

One Monday morning in 1838, Fred left home early. He did not go to work, though. He went to Stanley's room. When he came out, he was a handsome sailor, ready for travel.

Fred knew that blacks were checked carefully at train stations. He timed his arrival for the last minute. The engine chugged. Fred dashed up and jumped on the train as it began to move.

"So far, so good," Fred told himself.

He knew the dangers ahead, though. Suppose someone on the train knew him? Suppose the conductor saw that the description on Stanley's paper did not match him?

Luckily the train was crowded. The conductor had to work fast. "Where is your ticket?" he asked Fred.

"I was too late to get one, sir. I'll pay for it now."

"I suppose you have your free papers with you?"

Fred spoke boldly. "Well, sir, I have a paper with an American eagle on it. That will carry me anywhere."

The conductor looked quickly at the paper and gave it back.

Fred was still not safe. Every time the train stopped for more passengers, he held his breath. At one station he looked up and his heart jumped. A German blacksmith who knew Fred well came aboard. The two looked into each other's eyes for a long moment. Then the blacksmith went on to the next car.

"He knows I'm running away," Fred thought. "And he's letting me go."

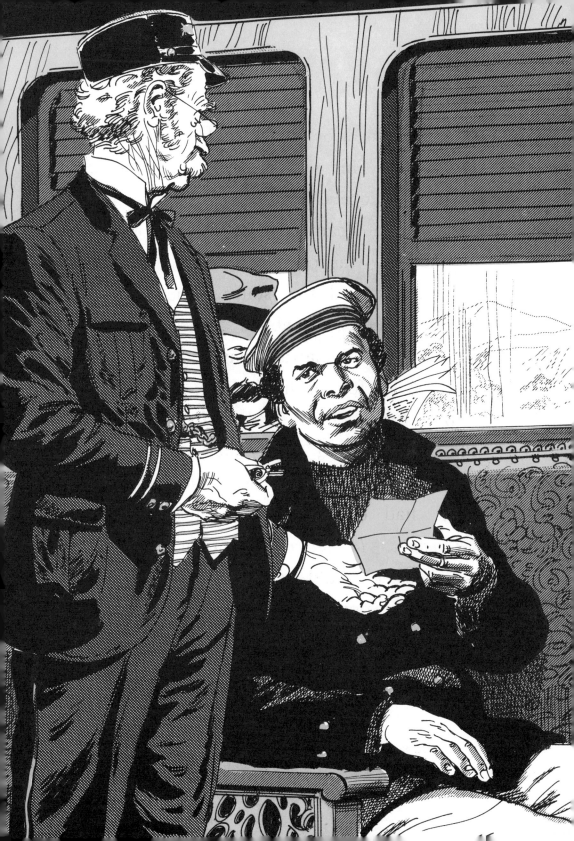

The train soon reached Wilmington, Delaware. This was a danger spot for Fred. Passengers had to leave the train and take a steamboat for Philadelphia. Wilmington was on the border between slave states and free states. The slave-catchers were all about. These spies searched for runaway slaves. Masters paid them for each slave caught.

But Fred's luck held. He reached Philadelphia and took another train. The next morning he was in New York.

He had escaped. Fred later wrote, *"A new world had opened upon me."*

But where could he go? Fred walked the streets until night. Then he crept behind some barrels on the waterfront. He slept soundly, the sweet sleep of freedom.

## Chapter 6

# New Name—New Life

Once again a friendly sailor helped Fred. The sailor took him to the home of David Ruggles, a young black.

Ruggles listened to Fred's story. "You'll have to hide," he said. "There are some slave-catchers even in the North. I'll hide you here while we send for Anna."

"But we are strangers," Fred said. "Why are you helping us?"

Ruggles smiled. "I am free and well educated. So I work to help others get their freedom. Do you know about the Underground Railroad?"

"Very little, sir."

Ruggles explained. "More and more slaves began escaping to free states. Their masters were puzzled. How could they suddenly disappear? Who helped them? One statesman said, 'They go as if swallowed up by an underground road.' So the secret system of helping slaves travel to freedom became known as the Underground Railroad."

"And you help these runaways, Mr. Ruggles?"

"Yes. We are called *conductors*. Our homes are the *stations*. We hide the slaves in our cellars, attics, and barns.

We guide them from station to station until they reach freedom. Some settle in northern cities, where the abolitionists help to keep them safe from slave-catchers. Others go to Canada. Slave-catchers cannot kidnap them there. Canada does not allow slavery."

Anna came and she and Fred were married. Ruggles told them his plans. "I'll send you to a friend in New Bedford, Massachusetts. That's a busy seaport and Fred can find work."

In New Bedford the couple went to the home of Nathan Johnson, a free black. "We'll help you get settled," Johnson said. "But first you must have a new name. Then your owner cannot trace you." Johnson looked at Fred's tall, proud figure and smiled. "I know.

I'm reading a book called *The Lady of the Lake*. There's a brave man in it named Douglass. That name fits you."

"*Douglass.*" Fred whispered the name. "*Frederick Douglass.*" He said it louder. "That's a grand name for a new life."

Fred and Anna rented a small house. Then Fred went to the shipyard. "I am a first-class shipworker," he told the owner. "I see you need help."

"I'm sorry," the owner answered him. "The workers won't let us hire blacks."

Fred was stunned. "I'll show them," he told Anna. "I'm young, I'm strong, and I'm my own master. Nothing can stop me now."

Fred dug cellars, swept chimneys and loaded ships. No job was too hard. Later, he got work in a factory.

In New Bedford, Fred read his first copy of the *Liberator*. This newspaper was trying to help end slavery.

The editor of the *Liberator* was William Lloyd Garrison. One day Garrison came to New Bedford to speak. He preached that all men were brothers. Garrison became Douglass' hero.

Abolitionists like Garrison belonged to groups that fought slavery. One group planned a big meeting in Nantucket, Massachusetts, in 1841.

"How I would like to go!" Douglass told Anna.

"Take a holiday," Anna begged. "You've never had one in your life."

Douglas went to Nantucket. He did not dream that the meeting would change his life.

*Chapter* 7

# The Young Orator

Hundreds of people came to the meeting. Douglass sat near the back of the hall. One of the abolitionists came over. "We want you to say a few words, Mr. Douglass."

"Me? Oh, no!"

"Please! Tell us about slavery."

Douglass trembled as he moved to the platform. He had never spoken to a group of white people before.

The faces were friendly. "What a handsome man!" some people whispered.

Douglass was over six feet tall and straight as an arrow. Black curly hair swept back from his broad forehead.

Garrison touched his arm gently. "Tell us your story, Frederick."

The words came easily once Douglass got started. He told how slaves prayed and sang about freedom. The audience hung on every word. *"Go on! Go on!"* they cried. Many wept.

When Douglass finished, Garrison stood up. *"Have we been listening to a thing, a piece of property, or to a man?"*

*"A man! A man!"* Everyone stood up and shouted.

"Come and travel with us," the abolitionists begged Douglass after the meeting. "Make speeches. Tell people how slavery *really* is."

Douglass and Anna were overjoyed. "Go with them," she said. "I have our babies for company." They now had a girl and a boy, Rosetta and Lewis.

Douglass read books and practiced hard to become a good speaker. He knew his new job would take skill and courage. Even in the North, many people felt that the abolitionists were stirring up trouble. Abolitionists were beaten, jailed and even killed.

One night Douglass was in a western town. The townspeople would not let him speak in a public building. That did not stop him. He spoke from a platform at the edge of the woods. A crowd came. What a wonderful actor and storyteller he was! He made people laugh one minute and cry the next.

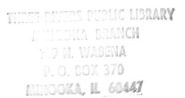

His deep-set eyes flashed like fire, and his voice thundered like a trumpet.

Suddenly 30 men dashed up, waving clubs. An egg hit Douglass' face. A brick crashed against his shoulder. "Kill him!" someone shouted. The mob beat Douglass and broke his hand. They left him lying on the ground.

Kind friends nursed Douglass until he was well. He was beaten time and time again. But nothing stopped him from speaking out against slavery.

Douglass became such a good speaker that some people began to say, "He was never a slave. He is only pretending."

To stop such talk, Douglass wrote the story of his life: *Narrative of the Life of Frederick Douglass, an American Slave.* In it he named his former owner.

That caused trouble for him. The Aulds demanded that their slave be returned.

"Leave the country at once," friends begged. "Hurry!"

Douglass escaped to England a few hours before slave-catchers came for him.

In England, Ireland and Scotland big crowds came to hear him whenever he spoke. "Stay with us," the English begged. "Send for your family."

Douglass thanked them. "America is my home. I must go back and help to end slavery."

English friends collected $700 to pay Hugh Auld for Douglass' freedom. They collected $2,100 to help Douglass with his work.

After 21 months, Douglass returned home, a free man.

# Chapter *8*

# "The North Star"

The small room on Buffalo Street buzzed with excitement. Douglass sat at a desk in one corner. A printing press and cases of type filled most of the room.

Douglass' three oldest children worked with him. Rosetta, now eleven, checked a list of names. Lewis and Frederick, Jr., helped two printers set type.

"Do we have any new customers?" Douglass asked Rosetta.

Rosetta's big eyes were bright with happiness. "Five, Father. People are really buying our newspaper."

Later, Anna came in with the two youngest children.

"We brought you some lunch," little Charles sang out.

Baby Annie ran over to her father and kissed him. She was only two, and the pet of the family. Douglass loved her dearly.

Lewis brought over a newspaper. "Look! Here's our first copy for this week."

Douglass took the paper. He read the name printed in big type at the top: *The North Star.*

Douglass' big dream had come true. He had used the money his English friends collected to start a newspaper. He had moved his family to Rochester, New York. "I'll fight slavery with my pen, as well as with my voice," Douglass said. "This paper will help to lead blacks out of slavery."

He thought of the runaway slaves who knew nothing about the geography of the country. The North Star led them toward free states. Often they sang:

*"I kept my eye on the bright*
*North Star,*
*And thought of liberty."*

So Douglass named his newspaper *The North Star*. It came out once a week. All the family helped with the paper. *The North Star* gave blacks hope.

It told of slaves escaping to freedom, and of friends working to end slavery. It printed stories and poems by black writers.

Douglass used *The North Star* to help all people who were fighting for equal rights. In those days, women did not get the same schooling as men. They could not hold government offices, and they could not vote.

A group of women began to speak for more equality. Most men laughed at them. They called men who helped the women "Aunt Nancy Men." But Douglass was not afraid to help.

In 1848, Douglass went to one of their meetings. Their leader said, "We want the right to vote." Her name was Mrs. Stanton.

"That's going too far," other women told her.

Mrs. Stanton whispered to Douglass, "Help me. They will listen to you."

Douglass made a speech. His voice flowed over the room like the music of an organ. "Slavery for women is as bad **as slavery for blacks.**"

The women cheered. "We want votes for women!"

Douglass spoke and wrote for many years. Once he made a speech before the New York Legislature. One of the legislators whispered to his friend, *"I would give twenty thousand dollars, if I could deliver that address in that manner."*

# Chapter *9*

# Railroad Running in Rochester

Songs filled the summer evening. A crowd of children sat in the front room of Douglass' big house on Alexander Street. Rosetta played the piano. Douglass played the violin. Everyone joined in the singing. Then Douglass taught two boys to whistle through their fingers.

Douglass loved children. He loved music, and had taught himself to play the violin. He said, *"No man can be an enemy of mine who loves the violin."*

Later that night, Douglass heard a rapping at the window, *rat-tat-tat.*

"Who's there?" he asked.

*"A friend with friends."*

This was the secret greeting of the Underground Railroad conductors. They sent messages in code and sign language.

A boy stood outside. "Good evening, Mr. Douglass. My father sent a barrel of apples."

"Where are the apples?"

"In our farm wagon."

The "apples" were really runaway slaves. Two teenage boys came in, their hats pulled down around their ears.

"We've been walking and hiding for a week," one said.

Douglass took them to a secret room. His whole family was now awake. When the runaways took off their hats, everyone was surprised.

"We're really girls," the runaways explained. "We knew that the slave-catchers would hunt for two girls. So we cut our hair and dressed as boys."

"Come, Rosetta," Anna said. "They need food."

The Douglass home was an important Underground Railroad station. Rochester was on Lake Ontario just across from Canada. Douglass' family helped in running the Railroad, just as they helped in running the paper.

The work had to be done in secret.

The government had passed a strict slave law. Anyone caught helping runaway slaves could be fined or put in prison.

The next day, the two oldest Douglass boys collected money and clothes to help the runaways. That night, they took them on to the next station.

Their father was worried about the millions of slaves still in the South. He made friends with a man named John Brown who worried about them too.

Brown often visited the Douglass family. Gentle Annie called him her second father. She followed him around, and sat on his knee to listen to stories.

Brown believed that slaves could hide in the mountains of Virginia. But first they must be freed. *"God has sent me to free the slaves,"* Brown decided.

One night in 1859 Brown sent for Douglass. "It's time for action!" Brown began. He unrolled a map. "This is the spot. I can get guns there. I'll need guns to arm the slaves."

"No! No!" Douglass cried. "That's Harper's Ferry, the government arsenal. You'll be killed." Douglass talked a day and a night. Nothing could make Brown change his mind.

*"Come with me, Douglass,"* Brown pleaded. *"I will defend you with my life."*

"No, friend. I must fight slavery in my own way."

Brown understood. The two friends parted sadly.

Brown and his followers, among them his own sons, did capture the arsenal.

But all of them were killed or taken prisoner. Brown was hanged for plotting against the government.

Letters showed that Douglass knew some of Brown's plans. Again Douglass escaped to England to save his life. But sad news brought him home again. His darling Annie was heartbroken over Brown's death. She worried about what might happen to her father. She lost the power to speak. Soon she died.

"The light and life of my house is gone," Douglass cried. The deaths of Brown and Annie made him hate slavery more than ever.

Brown became a hero to many. The time for action *had* come. Abraham Lincoln was President. The Civil War between the North and the South began.

# Chapter *10*

# "A Day for Poetry and Song"

January 1, 1863, was a cold, snowy day in Boston, Massachusetts. Douglass waited there for news from the White House. Would President Lincoln sign the Emancipation Proclamation? This act would free the slaves.

Northern cities were holding big celebrations. Boston held the biggest one. Douglass met with the crowd in a large hall. Messengers stayed at the telegraph office to bring the news. All day the crowd waited. No news came.

Darkness fell. Hours passed—eight, nine, ten o'clock. The people began to say, "Lincoln has changed his mind." Douglass tried to cheer them.

Suddenly a messenger ran inside. *"It's coming. It's on the wires."*

The people sprang to their feet. A second messenger waved a telegram. Lincoln *had* signed the Proclamation. The crowd went wild. Cheers and tears mixed with shouts and sobs.

"Free! Free at last!"

Douglass cried and shouted with them. His rich voice finally turned the shouting into singing: *"The year of jubilee is come!"*

No one wanted to sleep that night. The celebration went on till dawn. In fact, it went on for the whole year.

Douglass spoke at hundreds of joyful jubilee meetings. "We must help the Union win the war," he said.

"Let blacks fight," Douglass begged the government. The Army finally agreed. Douglass traveled from city to city to get black troops.

"I'll sign up," his son Charles said. "I want to be first."

"I'll be second," Lewis said. Later, Fred, Jr., joined too.

In May, 1863, 1,000 black troops marched down the streets of Boston. It was a proud day for Douglass.

But Douglass became angry when he found that black soldiers got less pay than white soldiers. They got little care as prisoners, and no promotions to better jobs.

"I must see President Lincoln at once," Douglass said. He went to the White House.

Lincoln smiled and held out his hand. It was the beginning of a true friendship. Lincoln often asked Douglass for advice when he planned for the blacks. "*My friend Douglass,*" Lincoln called him.

The war ended. But soon afterward, President Lincoln was killed. Later, Douglass received one of Lincoln's walking sticks, with a note from Mrs. Lincoln. "My husband often spoke of sending you a gift of friendship." Douglass treasured the gift more than any he received from famous people.

Friends asked Douglass, "Will you **stop and rest now? Blacks are free.** You have been fighting for 25 years."

"The fight is only beginning," he told them. "**Blacks must have full citizenship** and the right to vote. Schools, churches, colleges must be opened to all."

Some said, "**But blacks are not ready for this equality.**"

"*We* are ready," Douglass thundered. "**It is you who are not.**"

*Chapter* **11**

# The Sage of Anacostia

March 4, 1881, was an exciting day in Washington, D. C. James A. Garfield was the new President of the United States. Thousands of people lined the streets to see him.

Garfield stood in front of the Capitol building and took the oath of office. He gave a speech. A tall man stood beside him. The man's hair and beard were snow white, but his figure was straight and proud.

"That's Marshal Douglass," the people whispered.

Frederick Douglass had been given the job of Marshal for the District of Columbia. One of his duties was to escort the new President when he took office.

Douglass and Anna had moved to Washington, D.C. Their children were married and had children of their own. Douglass bought a 20-room house in Anacostia, overlooking the Potomac River and the dome of the Capitol. He called his home "Cedar Hill" because of the many cedar trees. It is now part of the park system in Washington.

Douglass was still busy. He wrote and spoke for the Irish and Chinese of America who were treated unfairly.

He worked to help poor people. He even helped to get better treatment for animals. "I have worked hardest to get **equal rights for blacks,**" he said. "But this does not keep me from working to help people of all races."

In 1882, Anna died. She had been too shy to travel with her famous husband. But she helped him in everything he did.

Later, Douglass married Helen Pitts, the daughter of an old American family. Helen helped him with his work. When he became Ambassador to Haiti, she went with him.

Douglass called his later life "The Golden Years." He spent happy days at Cedar Hill, writing letters and articles. In the evenings, friends came to visit.

He often played the violin, while Helen played the piano. Sometimes the two danced the Virginia reel. Friends said, "Douglass seems youthful for the first time in his life."

Hundreds of blacks wrote to Douglass for advice. They brought their problems to him and called him "The Sage of Anacostia." A sage is a wise man.

Douglass was happy to see young blacks growing up to become leaders. Blacks were now citizens. They could vote. Many were getting good schooling. Douglass told them, "Believe in America. Liberty, justice and fair play will win out in the end."

On February 20, 1895, the Women's Council held a meeting in Washington.

When Douglass came into the hall, the women all stood and waved white handkerchiefs. "Douglass! Douglass!"

That evening, Douglas was telling Helen about the meeting. Suddenly he sank to his knees and died. He was buried in Rochester, where he had run his Railroad and his *North Star*.

To blacks, and to many other people too, Douglass had been the North Star, holding out hope of freedom and equality.

Theodore Tilton, a famous poet-editor, wrote a book of poems about Douglass. Tilton said:

> *"I knew the noblest giants*
> *of my day,*
> *And he was of them."*